KINGFISHER KNOWLEDGE

PIRATES & SMUGGLERS

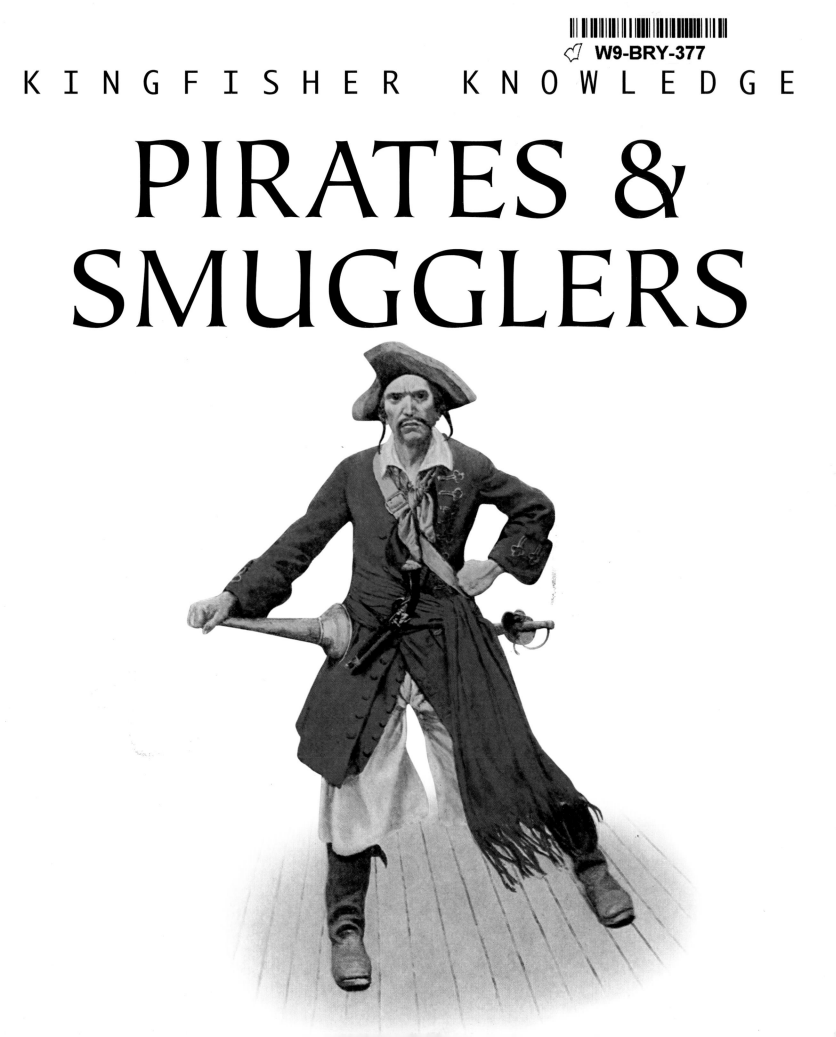

▼ A pirate attack was a truly bloodcurdling experience for sailors in the 1600s and 1700s. In this painting by the American artist Frederick Judd Waugh (1861–1940) a vicious gang of buccaneers (see pages 20–21) rushes on board an enemy ship, which is heavily armed with pistols and razor-sharp cutlasses. Not many crews put up a fight in the face of such a terrifying assault.

KINGFISHER KNOWLEDGE

PIRATES & SMUGGLERS

Moira Butterfield

Foreword by
Captain Stephen Bligh

KINGFISHER

BOSTON

Editor: Russell Mclean
Coordinating editor:
  Stephanie Pliakas
Designer: Carol Ann Davis
Consultant (illustrations):
  Gillian Hutchinson,
  National Maritime Museum
DTP manager: Nicky Studdart
DTP operator: Primrose Burton
Senior production controller:
  Lindsey Scott
Picture researcher: Rachael Swann
Indexer: Sue Lightfoot

KINGFISHER
a Houghton Mifflin Company imprint
222 Berkeley Street
Boston, Massachusetts 02116
www.houghtonmifflinbooks.com

First published in hardcover in 2005
First published in paperback in 2008
10 9 8 7 6 5 4 3 2 1

1TR/1107/TWP/MA(MA)/130ENSOMA/F

LIBRARY OF CONGRESS CATALOGING-IN-PUBLICATION DATA
Butterfield, Moira, 1961–
Pirates and smugglers/Moira Butterfield.—1st ed.
 p. cm.—(Kingfisher knowledge)
 Includes index.
 1. Pirates—Juvenile literature.
 2. Smuggling—Juvenile literature.
 3. Privateering—Juvenile literature.
 4. Smugglers—Juvenile literature. I. Title.
 II. Series.
 G535.B94 2005
 910.4'5—dc22
 2005007406

ISBN 978-0-7534-6248-5

Printed in Singapore

► Today's pirates use small, fast boats to outrun
their prey. These bandits are based in the Riau
islands of Indonesia. Once they have caught up
with their target, the pirates use a long bamboo
pole with a hook at the end to pull their own
boat alongside it before boarding.

Contents

GO FURTHER . . .
INFORMATION PANEL KEY:

 Web sites and
further reading

career paths

places to visit

NOTE TO READERS
The Web site addresses listed in this
book are correct at the time of publishing.
However, due to the ever-changing nature of the
Internet, Web site addresses and content can change.
Web sites can contain links that are unsuitable for children.
The publisher cannot be held responsible for changes in Web site addresses
or content or for information obtained through third-party Web sites. We
strongly advise that Internet searches are supervised by an adult.

Foreword

Given my namesake, Captain William Bligh of *HMS Bounty* fame, some would say it was inevitable that one day I would become the chief executive of the Maritime and Coastguard Agency in the United Kingdom. Like William Bligh, I sailed as a ship's captain for more than 20 years. Unlike William Bligh, I never suffered a mutiny, and, I am pleased to say, neither did I come into contact with any pirates.

Whether it is Robert Louis Stevenson's character Long John Silver of 1881's *Treasure Island* or Captain Jack Sparrow in the Hollywood blockbuster movie *Pirates of the Caribbean*, we tend to associate pirates with not doing any real harm, living just beyond the rule of law, in search of treasures.

However, as you will see, the history of piracy and smuggling has had its fair share of scoundrels. From Captain Morgan and Blackbeard to the female pirates Anne Bonny and Mary Read, piracy has never been short of bloodcurdling characters, and you will no doubt enjoy reading about their adventures.

Movies and novels have helped paint a picture of pirates as lovable rogues. But, in reality, piracy and smuggling was a cutthroat existence. Many innocent people lost their lives at the hands of pirates who would do anything for money, whether it was murder, theft, or—in the case of the Napoleonic wars—betraying the nation by selling secrets and hiding French spies.

Smuggling is particularly important to the Maritime and Coastguard Agency because the original coast guard began as a response to smugglers who operated in the seas around Great Britain. In the 1700s and 1800s coast guards lived alongside smuggling every day—either trying to stop it or because the local community was connected with the trade.

Thankfully those terrifying days around the British coast have passed, but piracy remains a huge problem in other parts of the world, especially in the South China Sea and the Strait of Malacca, parts of the Caribbean and South America, west and east Africa, and the Indian Ocean. Swashbuckling swords have been replaced by guns as pirates target important shipping lanes. This modern activity threatens international trade, national economies, and, most importantly, seafarers' lives.

Far from being harmless, modern pirates cause havoc and fear, and there is increasing evidence that piracy is linked to terrorism. Not only is the number of armed robberies at sea growing but so is the threat of terrorists boarding and hijacking ships with the goal of attacking other ships and even the environment. Drug smuggling and terrorism are a far cry from searching for treasures on desert islands.

Piracy is as relevant today as it has always been. It is wonderful that this book outlines not only the rich history of piracy and smuggling but also the modern-day threat that still exists. I hope you will enjoy the read.

Captain Stephen Bligh
Chief Executive, Maritime and Coastguard Agency, U.K.

CHAPTER 1

The first pirates

Think of a pirate, and you probably imagine a flamboyant man wearing a long coat, with a cutlass and maybe a peg leg and an eye patch. This image is based on pirates of the 1700s, but that is just one era in the long and violent history of piracy.

For thousands of years people have sailed the oceans carrying valuable goods to sell in different countries. Pirates have roamed the seas for just as long, attacking ships and coastal towns for profit.

The ancient Egyptians suffered attacks by "sea peoples" as far back as the 1200s B.C. The ancient Greeks and Romans faced pirates too. And as sea trade developed in medieval times, so did the threat of oceangoing crime.

Mosaic showing the ancient Greek god Dionysus, in the form of a lion, driving pirates from his ship (see page 8)

Ancient times

From around 2500 B.C., great civilizations developed around the Mediterranean. The sea was used more and more to transport goods such as grains and olive oil. Merchant ships sailed close to the shore because the sailors feared the open sea. They ran the risk of being ambushed by pirates, however, who lurked along the coast, ready to attack a passing vessel and steal its valuable cargo.

People stealers

In ancient times the slave trade was a big business. Mediterranean pirates could make a profit by kidnapping people from coastal settlements and selling them into slavery. Wealthy prisoners were sold back to their families for a large ransom. A story in Greek mythology tells about a pirate gang that captured Dionysus, the god of wine (see page 7). When Dionysus changed into a lion, the bandits jumped overboard in fright. As a punishment, the god turned the pirates into a school of dolphins.

▶ In the Mediterranean Sea a pirate galley attacks a merchant ship carrying its valuable cargo of grains from Egypt to Rome in Italy. Cargo vessels were heavy, slow, and powered by only the wind. They were no match for the sleek, fast ships that the pirates used. To sink enemy vessels, galleys were armed with a battering ram. This was a wooden beam, strengthened with brass, that stuck out from the front of the ship.

Roman merchant ship

Most merchant vessels had small crews and few weapons.

◀ As a young man, Julius Caesar (100–44 B.C.) was captured and held hostage by Cilician pirates. After his ransom was paid, Caesar was set free. In revenge, he hunted the pirates and had them executed.

This illustration from a Greek vase dates back to the mid-6th century B.C. It shows an example of the navy warships that the Greeks built to fight Mediterranean pirates.

Pirates prove useful

The seas around Greece are full of inlets and islands, which made ideal pirate hideouts. Piracy became a big problem for the ancient Greeks, who built fleets of warships to fight back. Sometimes the Greek city-states went to war with one another, however, and then the Greek leaders encouraged pirates to attack enemy ships. This is an early example of rulers deliberately using pirates to harm their enemies.

Romans versus pirates

As the Roman Empire grew in power, it set out to crush the pirates of the Mediterranean. First they were driven eastward. By the 1st century B.C., Cilicia, an area of what is now Turkey, had become the center of piracy. The bandits threatened Rome's vital grain supply from Egypt, so in 67 B.C. the famous soldier Pompey the Great (106–48 B.C.) attacked their bases from sea and land, wiping out the pirates.

Pirate galley

Once the boats were locked together, well-armed pirates would swarm onto the cargo ship.

◄ Galleys were used by both pirates and navies in ancient times. The basic design was Greek in origin and was copied by the Romans. The galleys carried a sail, but they were mostly powered by two or three sets of oarsmen. This made them fast and easy to maneuver alongside a cargo vessel.

Wooden fighting turret

Some pirate galleys had eyes painted on the prow (front) as a good-luck charm and to make the ship look more impressive.

Oarsmen inside the galley provided ramming power.

▼ A fleet of Viking warships, or longboats, speeds toward the coast of northeastern England, ready to raid a Christian church of its metal treasures. The earliest recorded Viking attack in England was on the monastery of Lindisfarne Island in A.D. 793. When they raided, the Vikings also grabbed people to ransom or to sell as slaves.

Longboats had a shallow depth, making them easy to land on a beach or row up a river.

Powerful oarsmen, ready to join the attack

Steering oar

The northern menace

From the A.D. 400s, the Roman Empire crumbled, and for the next few hundred years piracy spread once again. In northern Europe barbarians raided ships and coastal settlements mercilessly, striking fear into ordinary people with their lightning-quick attacks and violence.

Overlapping wooden planks, hammered together with iron nails, made the longboats strong enough to sail on the open seas.

Viking raiders

The Vikings of Scandinavia were the most feared of the northern raiders. From the A.D. 700s–1000s, they menaced the coasts of northern Europe. The Vikings were expert sailors who could travel far across the open sea and then sail up rivers, taking towns and villages by surprise. Before the inhabitants could hide their valuables, fierce warriors would swarm ashore to kill and steal.

The Vikings measured their wealth by the amount of precious metal that they owned. They liked to raid Christian monasteries and churches because of the metal treasures they would often find there. The Vikings stole large quantities from churches, much of which was melted down to be made into jewelry or metal bars. Sometimes they simply cut up the treasures into pieces to use as money.

The pirate monk

England and France were often at war during the Middle Ages, and both nations could turn a blind eye to piracy when it harmed the enemy. One pirate was a former priest, Eustace the Monk (c. 1170–1217). Under the protection of King John of England (ruled 1199–1216), he raided French ships in the English Channel. Then he switched sides and was paid by the French to attack England. He was captured by the English and was beheaded on board his own ship.

Baltic barbarians

The Baltic Sea was an area of great trading importance in the 1300s. Many large ports joined together to create a trading group called the Hanseatic League, and their well-stocked ships became pirate targets. One of the most famous bandits was Klaus Störtebeker. He terrorized the Baltic during the 1390s but was finally captured by a Hanseatic fleet in 1402. The pirate and 70 of his followers were taken to Hamburg, Germany, and executed.

▲ The name of the Baltic pirate Störtebeker (died 1402) means "down in one gulp." To join his crew, a sailor had to pass an unusual test—to drink an enormous beaker of beer in one swallow.

Slave pirates

In the 1400s and 1500s north Africa was ruled by the Turkish Ottoman Empire. Muslim pirates, called corsairs, set sail from ports along the Mediterranean coast to attack Christian trading ships and settlements. The corsairs were looking for valuable goods—Christians to sell as slaves. Over a period of 200 years up to one million Europeans are thought to have been kidnapped and enslaved. The corsairs were called barbarians by their Christian enemies—or Barbary pirates for short.

▲ Corsair leaders, such as the Barbarossa brothers, became extremely wealthy, with their own palaces and powerful galley fleets. This painting shows Khayr ad-Din (c. 1470–1546), the youngest brother. As young men, they were given the nickname "Barbarossa" because it described their red beards.

The pirate coast
The north African cities of Algiers, Tunis, and Tripoli were the corsair strongholds and were also the locations of the slave markets that the pirates supplied. Famous corsair captains included the Barbarossa brothers and Murat Rais (c. 1535–1638), who sailed as far as Ireland to raid coastal villages, kidnapping everyone and leaving entire areas deserted. But not all of the corsairs were Arabs. Some Christian sailors "turned Turk" and joined in the lucrative slave snatching.

Corsair galleys
The corsairs used sleek, fast galleys with oars and triangular sails to outrun their prey. The oars were pulled by naked slaves, who were bullied and whipped into rowing faster by Muslim soldiers called Janissaries. The front of a galley was armed with a cannon, so it could fire forward at the enemy while presenting a very narrow target for return fire. Once a galley had caught up with the enemy, the armed Janissaries would swarm on board for hand-to-hand battle.

◀ Christian priests (shown here on the left) often tried to buy back slaves from the corsairs, who sold them at slave markets along the Barbary coast.

Slaves for sale

Muslim corsairs sold their captives in the thriving slave markets of the north African coast or forced them to row in their galleys. The life of a galley slave was brief and brutal, so new slaves were always needed. Female captives were usually sold into harems. At one time there were said to be so many Christian slaves in Algiers that you could buy one for the cost of an onion.

▼ This painting, from A.D. 1670, shows a fleet of Dutch merchant ships being attacked by Barbary corsairs. One of the corsair galleys is in the foreground. Corsairs on the bow (front) and stern (rear) aim arrows at a Dutch vessel. Galleys were sleek and fast, capable of sudden bursts of high speed for as long as the slave oarsmen could stand it.

Pirate knights

Muslim corsairs and merchant ships were regularly attacked by Christian sailors led by the Knights of St. John—an alliance set up to fight the corsairs' religion of Islam. At first the knights were backed by Christian rulers, but eventually they turned to piracy. The Muslim slaves who rowed their galleys were treated just as brutally as the Christians who suffered at the hands of the Barbary pirates.

Plundering privateers

In the 1500s European nations competed to conquer new lands and bring back profitable cargoes. At the forefront of exploration was Spain, with valuable colonies in the Caribbean, Central America, and South America. Spain was a powerful Catholic country, and its Protestant enemies tried to disrupt Spanish trade by hiring private sea captains to attack on their behalf. These licensed pirates were called privateers.

▼ Sir John Hawkins (1532–1595) was a hero to the English because he raided Spanish ships and fought the Armada in 1588. But to others, he was a criminal who started the slave trade between Africa and the Americas by illegally selling west African slaves to the Spanish colonies.

Letters of marque
European rulers issued letters of marque—formal contracts by which the monarch would hire a privately owned ship and its crew and then send it to disrupt enemy sea trade. A letter of marque authorized acts of piracy and ensured that the monarch took a share of any cargo that was seized. It was a cheap way to wage war and make a large profit at the same time.

Built for speed
Privateer ships were sleeker and faster than the sturdy Spanish treasure ships, or galleons (see pages 16–17). They used cannons to batter a galleon into submission, avoiding the risk of a hand-to-hand fight on board.

Privateer heroes

European rulers rewarded privateers well. Francis Drake (1540–1596) was knighted by Queen Elizabeth I (ruled 1558–1603) for attacking Spanish ships in the 1570s. In 1588 a large Spanish fleet called the Armada set sail to invade England. Privateers such as Drake and John Hawkins helped defeat the fleet and became national heroes. More than 100 years later René Duguay-Trouin was honored by the French king Louis XIV for his attacks against the English.

Privateers turn pirates

The seagoing nations of Europe were not always at war during the 1500s. But even though the privateers were licensed to act only in wartime, this did not stop them from attacking ships during times of peace. The lure of big profits was just too big. Queen Elizabeth I would often turn a blind eye to the peacetime activities of her privateers, whom she called "sea dogs." Privately, she even supported their attacks, which brought her great wealth.

▼ Privateers helped defeat the Spanish Armada. They used their seamanship and knowledge of the English coastline to outsmart the enemy, although the weather also helped them.

▶ French privateers were called corsairs. René Duguay-Trouin (1673–1736), the most well-known corsair, captured 16 warships and around 300 merchant vessels during his 23-year career.

◄ These Spanish coins came from the wreck of a pirate ship called the *Whydah* (see page 58). Maybe they were stolen from a Spanish treasure galleon.

BAHAMAS

Havana

GULF OF MEXICO

CUBA

Santiago de Cuba

The Spanish Main

The area known as the Spanish Main included the Spanish colonies of the Caribbean, Central America, and the northern shores of South America. The wealth of the Spanish Main became legendary, and the galleons that carried the treasures back to Spain were the leading targets for privateers during the 1500s.

JAMAICA

Port Royal

○ Belize

CENTRAL AMERICA

Lands of treasures

In the 1520s and 1530s Spanish conquerors, known as conquistadores, brutally overthrew the Aztec and Inca nations of Central and South America. The Spanish ruthlessly stole the locals' wealth and discovered large reserves of precious metals. Using slaves from both the local area and west Africa, they mined huge quantities of silver, which they sent back to Spain by sea.

The journey home

Individual ships were vulnerable to attacks, so the Spanish found safety in large numbers. Once each year an enormous fleet of up to 100 ships would set out to transport the treasures home. Although sturdy and well defended, the Spanish galleons were often slow and difficult to sail. Eagle-eyed privateers cruised the Main on the lookout for unprotected treasure ships that had been separated from the fleet by darkness or bad weather.

Cartagena

Portobelo

◀ The Spanish captured fantastic gold and silver treasures such as this Mexican gold figure. They melted down most of the metal to make coins. Silver coins were called pieces of eight, while gold coins were known as doubloons.

▶ This painting shows pirates in a small boat about to board a slow, heavily laden treasure galleon in the Caribbean.

Tortuga

HISPANIOLA

Santo Domingo

Isla Vaca (Cow Island)

Lumbering galleons

Galleons sailed well when the wind blew from behind but were much slower traveling against the wind, when they were most easily caught by privateers. Once a galleon had been chased down, a privateer would use cannon fire to try to force it to surrender. If hand-to-hand fighting broke out, the Spanish stood a better chance because they were well armed with muskets, rapiers, and knives.

Deadly pirate hunter

In the 1540s and 1550s Spanish galleons were attacked by French pirates based in what is now Florida. Spanish nobleman Pedro de Menendez de Avilés (1519–1574) was sent to hunt them down. In 1565 he seized the pirates' base at Fort Caroline while they were at sea. The inhabitants were slaughtered, and the pirates were executed when the Spaniard caught up with them.

▼ The Spanish Main was a vast geographical area centered around the many islands of the Caribbean such as Cuba and Hispaniola. This 16th-century map shows some of the major ports in the region.

Maracaibo

SOUTH AMERICA

TRINIDAD

The Vikings ransacked Christian churches because they were often full of valuable treasures such as this book with a jeweled cover.

Pirates prey on people

Pirates have brought terror to the oceans since seagoing trade began. For thousands of years they have preyed on ships carrying valuable cargo and have attacked coastal towns and villages.

From ancient times pirates were involved in seizing people. Ancient Greeks, Romans, Vikings, Barbary corsairs, and European privateers all made money from capturing and selling people as slaves, sometimes kidnapping them from their own homes, as well as from ships. Rich captives were ransomed back to families who could afford to rescue them, but poor people were sold for a high profit.

Rulers and pirates

From early times kings and queens have used pirates for their own purposes, supporting them by lending them ships, giving them permission to attack enemies, and often taking a share of the profits from their raids. In the 1500s the link between rulers and pirates was especially strong. European countries went to war for religious reasons and also to stop one another from trading overseas and colonizing new lands. Monarchs like England's Queen Elizabeth I encouraged pirates by handing out privateer licenses.

The Spanish Main

Central America, northern South America, and the islands of the Caribbean—the Spanish Main—were a hotbed of pirate activity during the 1500s. England and France sent privateers to the region to attack Spanish galleons, which were loaded with gold and silver treasures. The privateers became heroes in their own countries, but to others, they were seen as ruthless and violent criminals.

Go further . . .

To find out more about ships and pirates through the ages, visit the Web site of the National Maritime Museum in London, England: www.nmm.ac.uk

Read about the reconstruction of a Viking longship on the Web site of the Roskilde Viking Ship Museum: www.vikingeskibsmuseet.dk

The World of Pirates by Philip Steele (Kingfisher, 2004)

Life in Ancient Rome by Simon Adams (Kingfisher, 2005)

For younger readers:
The Kingfisher Treasury of Pirate Stories (Kingfisher, 2003)

Archaeologist
Studies the past by working on historical sites to reveal old ruins and objects without damaging them.

Archivist
Preserves and catalogs historical documents.

Curator
In charge of a museum area, ensuring that the exhibits are stored in an environment that will keep them safe and in good condition.

Preservationist
A highly trained technician who is a specialist in preserving historical objects, sometimes using special tools and chemicals.

Visit Rome, the capital of Italy, where you can see ruins and museums dedicated to ancient Roman life. The port area of ancient Rome was called Ostia.

Visit the reconstruction of Francis Drake's ship, the *Golden Hind* (exhibition open from March to October):
The Quay
Brixham TQ5 8AW, U.K.
Phone: +44 (0) 1803 856223
www.goldenhind.co.uk

A scene from a Hollywood movie, *Blackbeard the Pirate,* set at the time of the Golden Age

CHAPTER 2

The Golden Age

A fast, sleek pirate sloop glides out of the mist and up behind a lumbering merchant ship weighed down with precious cargo. A murderous pirate crew swarms aboard, led by a crazy captain.

This is a scene familiar from movies but also from eyewitness accounts written during the "Golden Age" of piracy—roughly between A.D. 1690 and 1730—when crime was at its height off the American coast and in the Indian Ocean. Writings of the time tell of extraordinary pirate characters such as the fearsome Blackbeard and the wily Captain Morgan. These villains became celebrities whose adventures scandalized and fascinated readers in Europe. Since then their true-life escapades have been mixed with the imaginations of writers to create the ever-popular image of the pirate.

Buccaneers

The Golden Age of piracy began with a ragged group of lawless hunters. For years the Spanish had tried to keep other countries away from the Caribbean, but in the early 1600s a group of French former sailors settled on the island of Hispaniola. They lived off the land, hunting wild cattle and preserving the meat in huts called smokehouses, or boucans. They became known as boucaniers—or buccaneers. When Spain tried to drive out the hunters, they turned to a life of piracy, attacking Spanish ships and coastal settlements.

▲ Buccaneers were notoriously cruel, especially Frenchman François L'Ollonais (1635–c. 1669). He was said to have ripped out the heart of a prisoner and stuffed it into another captive's mouth.

▼ Henry Morgan was a Welsh sea captain who became a buccaneer. His privateer's license meant that he had to pay the English monarch a share of any wealth that he captured at sea. To circumvent this rule, he often attacked coastal towns. Here, Morgan and his men loot the town of Portobelo, Panama, in 1668. They are trying to find out from a prisoner where a treasure might be hidden.

Pirate island

When the buccaneers were driven out of Hispaniola (present-day Haiti and the Dominican Republic), they settled on the nearby island of Tortuga (see map on page 17). Despite Spanish attempts to destroy the hideout, the number of buccaneers grew as the island attracted runaway slaves, French pirates, and fortune seekers.

Legends are born

Tortuga became one of the most infamous pirate bases in the Caribbean. It was run as a type of pirate republic, led by daring and vicious captains. We know a lot about them because of a book called *Bucaniers of America*, written by a pirate surgeon, Alexandre Exquemelin (1645–1707). He wrote about treasure raids, terrible cruelties, and lucky escapes. He explained how the buccaneers would return to Tortuga with their plunder to celebrate and plan more raids. His book was a bestseller in the 1600s, and it is the basis for many of our modern ideas about pirates.

The Welsh buccaneer

The English government at this time used pirates as an unofficial navy in order to capture land. It gave a privateer's license to Henry Morgan (c. 1635–1688), one of the most famous buccaneers. His raids on Spanish settlements during the 1660s yielded a fortune. He was knighted by the British and eventually became the governor of Jamaica in 1674.

Morgan's exploding ship

Henry Morgan had a fleet of ships that were loaned from the British. One night he held a meeting with his captains on board a warship called the *Oxford*. As the officers sat around the table, a stray spark—possibly from a musket being fired for fun or from a pig roast—ignited a barrel of gunpowder. It blew up and killed 350 men. Miraculously, Morgan escaped. The scattered wreck of the *Oxford* was located by divers in 2004 off the coast of Haiti.

▼ The French hunters used cutlasses to butcher the animals they caught on Hispaniola. The cutlass became a favorite pirate weapon because it was short and easy to carry. This illustration of a cutlass fight dates from 1685.

Blackbeard's time

As Europe became more peaceful in the late 1600s and early 1700s, the privateers of the Caribbean and American Atlantic coast lost their official support—but they continued being pirates because it was so profitable. Some, such as the notorious Blackbeard, persisted raiding cargo ships in the Caribbean. Others preyed on slave vessels along the west coast of Africa or sailed into the Indian Ocean to raid ships on trading routes from India and the Far East. The trip from the Americas to the Indian Ocean via Africa and back was known as the pirate round.

▶ The "pirate round" took ships from North America across the Atlantic to prey on slave ships off the west African coast near Guinea. Then they sailed around the Cape of Good Hope to raid vessels in the Indian Ocean before heading home.

▼ Edward Low (died 1724) was one of the cruelest pirates of Blackbeard's time. Legend says that he once cut off and cooked a man's lips. Here, one of Low's equally vicious crew members shoots a prisoner at point-blank range.

NORTH AMERICA

Ocracoke Creek, Blackbeard's lair

Gulf of Mexico

The Caribbean

ATLANTIC OCEAN

EUROPE

AFRICA

Route of the pirate round

Guinea coast

SOUTH AMERICA

N

Cape of Good Hope

Ships of the Golden Age

For long ocean voyages the pirates of the Golden Age preferred three-masted, square-sailed ships, usually vessels that they had captured. For shallow inshore waters small sloops were ideal. These were fast and easily maneuverable, with triangular sails attached to a bowsprit—a long wooden beam at the front of the ship. When their prey was sighted, the pirates would come up astern (from behind) to avoid the enemy's main cannon, which usually pointed sideways.

The infamous Blackbeard

Blackbeard (died 1718) is the most famous pirate of this era, although he operated for only two years. He was English, and his real name was probably Edward Teach. He cruised the Caribbean and the Gulf of Mexico in a captured French slave ship, seizing prizes and taking them to a hideout in Ocracoke Creek, off the coast of North Carolina. There, Blackbeard bribed the authorities to turn a blind eye to his activities and sold his booty to the locals.

Death of a legend

Blackbeard felt safe in the shallow waters of his Ocracoke lair. But late in 1718 the British governor of Virginia, fearing growing lawlessness, sent a Royal Navy expedition to find him. Led by Lieutenant Robert Maynard, the British took the pirate fleet by surprise, and in the bloody fight that followed, Blackbeard was killed. His head was hung from the bowsprit of Maynard's sloop (see page 32). Members of the legendary pirate's crew were captured and hanged.

▼ Blackbeard terrified his enemies. When he went into battle, burning fuses in his hair created a cloud of choking black smoke. He and his crew were often drunk on a cocktail of rum mixed with gunpowder, and it was even said that he killed members of his crew from time to time, just to show who was in charge.

ASIA

INDIAN OCEAN

Madagascar

KEY

Pirate hot spot

Pirate attacks

Nothing struck fear into the heart of a sailor as much as the sight of a group of desperate pirates, armed and dangerous, climbing over the side of his ship. Pirate captains had to employ a range of strategies in order to capture a prize successfully. They used stealth, deception, threats of violence, and, ultimately, overwhelming force to get their prey to surrender.

Bloody battles

During the late 1600s and early 1700s life at sea was especially dangerous for all sailors, both pirates and law-abiding seamen. Conditions were harsh, the sea was a dangerous place, and life expectancy was short. Pirates were notorious for showing no mercy to those who fought against them. Hand-to-hand battles were brutal and bloody, and many men on both sides could be killed in action.

Boarding tactics

Pirates preferred to frighten a ship into surrendering, but if they had to board, they threw grappling irons— metal hooks on the end of a long rope—into the rigging (ropes) of a treasure ship to pull it close to the pirate vessel. Tar grenades might be thrown to cause confusion—either by setting fire to rigging and sails or by creating thick smoke. Most seamen went barefoot, so spiked metal weapons, called caltrops, were thrown on deck to wound the treasure ship's defenders. Once the pirates had set foot on board, they attacked with cutlasses, pistols, muskets, axes, and daggers.

▲ Having softened up the enemy, pirates swarm up the steep wooden sides of a Spanish galleon in order to overwhelm the defending crew. Armed with swords and guns, the pirates are prepared to risk death for a rich prize.

◀ Movie pirates, such as Captain Jack Sparrow in *Pirates of the Caribbean*, usually wear a lot of jewelry. This is, in fact, true to history. Pirates of the Golden Age often dressed in fine clothes and jewelry stolen from wealthy captives. They liked to look like rich aristocrats as a way of flaunting their success.

▶ This action-packed scene shows the battle that killed Blackbeard (see page 23) in 1718. Cannons and gunfire added to the havoc during the fight. A cannonball smashing into a ship's deck could send deadly wooden shards flying everywhere, while swivel guns mounted on pivots could spray an enemy deck with gunshots.

Piracy or death

The defeated crew members were offered a choice—they could join the pirates or die. Not surprisingly, many turned to piracy. In some ways a pirate's life was better than an ordinary seaman's. Pirates had more freedom from authority, the chance to make a lot of money, and the prospect of drunken celebrations on a Caribbean island. When a naval officer was caught, the pirates soon found out how he had treated his men. If he had been cruel, he was given a taste of his own medicine.

Jolly Roger

The Jolly Roger, the skull-and-crossbones flag flying from the topmast of a ship, is the most well-known pirate symbol of all. Pirate flags were flown to warn ships that the bandits would kill anyone who opposed them. The name is thought to come from the French *jolie rouge* ("pretty red one") because pirate flags were originally blood red.

▲ Each pirate captain had his own flag, often decorated with symbols of death. Blackbeard's flag shows a skeleton holding an hourglass and pointing an arrow at a bleeding heart. The message is clear: "You don't have much time—surrender or die!"

Life on board

The thrill of chasing a prize did not come every day for pirates of the Golden Age. In between short bursts of fighting, pirates had to put up with long periods of boredom, exhausting chores to keep the ship in good condition, and terrible food. Even when there were no battles to be fought, a pirate's life was very dangerous, with a high risk of death by accident or disease.

▲ The many sails of a large 18th-century ship had to be kept in good condition at all times. Most crews had a sail maker who could repair ripped sails with a large needle. At sea, the sails could often be adjusted from the deck, but sometimes seamen had to scramble up the rigging (ropes) to tie the canvas sails to the wooden poles.

Food and drinks

Hardtack biscuits, made from flour and water, made up the largest part of many sailors' diets. On board, the biscuits soon became infested with weevils. Before eating them, sailors would tap the biscuits in order to knock out the weevils. Sometimes hens were kept on a ship, and the crew would also catch fish and turtles to eat. To drink, there were barrels of water and beer. Sailors often used alcohol to hide the bad taste of stale water.

Sores from scurvy

Fresh food quickly went rotten on board a ship, so most food had to be preserved by either smoking or salting. On long voyages many sailors suffered from a disease called scurvy, which is caused by a lack of fruits and vegetables. It left their teeth rotten and their skin covered in sores. In 1753 it was discovered that eating citrus fruits, such as limes and lemons, could prevent the disease.

▶ Pirate ships were cramped because captains had to take enough men to sail the vessels that they captured. A large ship, such as this one, might have more than 150 men on board. The pirate captain and his senior men had cabins at the stern (back) of the ship. The rest of the crew had no living quarters. Instead they hung hammocks wherever they could find space.

Surgery at sea

Ships of the Golden Age were so dirty that even minor illnesses or wounds could be life threatening. Most crews included a ship's surgeon, who often had no medical training at all. The usual treatment for an injured limb was to cut it off, with no painkiller except alcohol, which the patient drank to dull the pain. Because there were no antiseptics, the chances of dying from an infection after surgery were high.

The pirate code

Surprisingly for such cutthroat gangs, some pirate crews created strict codes of behavior to avoid fighting among the men. Often women and gambling were banned from the ship. Some of the measures were very advanced for their day. For example, crew members could vote on important matters. They also had the right to an equal share of stolen loot, and pirates who were wounded in action often received financial help.

▲ In the navy one of the harshest punishments was to be flogged (whipped) with a cat-o'-nine-tails—a whip with nine knotted tails. Victims were scarred for life or even died. Many pirates were former navy sailors who held grudges against their old officers. Some probably carried the scars of naval floggings. No wonder pirates often renamed their captured ships *The Revenge*.

KEY

1. Sailor on watch
2. Poop deck
3. Helmsman steering the ship
4. Captain's cabin
5. Food supplies
6. Sail room
7. Hull
8. Rudder
9. Keel
10. Cannon
11. Mainmast
12. Rowboat
13. Oarsmen
14. Cannonball supply
15. Water and beer barrels
16. Flogging on the forecastle
17. Anchor
18. Bowsprit

◀ A sailing ship's oars were used when there was no wind or when the ship was entering a port.

▶ Rats were unwelcome passengers on all types of ships at this time. They could cause great damage by eating food supplies and damaging equipment. They also carried serious diseases. On a long voyage the rats would breed, and thousands could end up on board, ruining the food supplies and gnawing the ropes and wood.

Pirates on land

Pirates did not spend all of their time at sea, and they looked forward to a riotous time on land as a reward for the hardships of life on the waves. Captains searched for a safe haven that could be fortified against attacks from the authorities and where their crew could spend money. In the Indian Ocean sparsely populated Madagascar was perfect, while the Caribbean was dotted with notorious pirate haunts such as Port Royal in Jamaica and the island of Tortuga.

▲ Because life at sea was often brutal and brief, many pirates felt that saving money for a comfortable retirement was a waste of time. They spent their money ashore, often gambling it away. This pack of 19th-century playing cards was confiscated from a captured pirate ship by a British naval officer.

Wildness on shore

Once pirates set foot on land, they looked for release from the boredom and dangers of life at sea. They had plenty of money to lavish on drinking, gambling, and entertaining women. Many pirates gained wealth beyond the dreams of ordinary sailors, but they also wasted it. Sometimes they would spend the equivalent, in today's money, of thousands of dollars in a single night. Drunkenness was widespread, with local Caribbean rum being the favorite drink.

The dream of Libertatia

A lot of information about pirates comes from Charles Johnson's book *A General History of Pyrates*, published in 1724. It mentions Captain Misson, who set up a pirate republic called Libertatia on the island of Madagascar. It was said to be democratic—all pirates were equal, and any loot was shared. Many historians dismiss Libertatia as a myth, but it is true that some pirates settled on Madagascar and that the pirate code was democratic.

Buried treasures

Possibly the most famous pirate myth is that hoards of captured treasures were buried on remote islands, ready to be tracked down later with a coded treasure map. There are many legends about hidden loot and rumors of pirate gold, but very little has been found—so it is possible that these tales have been exaggerated by storytellers.

Kidd's loot

One of the most famous treasure tales relates to Captain William Kidd (see page 33). He was licensed by the British authorities to hunt French pirates in the Indian Ocean. However, he also attacked British ships in order to boost his profits. He sailed to the east coast of North America and is said to have buried a fantastic treasure on Long Island, New York. As yet, no one knows the truth about Kidd's loot, although many have searched for it.

▲ The flag of Captain Bartholomew "Black Bart" Roberts (1682–1722) pictured a pirate drinking a jug of rum with a skeleton. Although Roberts is said to have preferred to drink tea, his men were certainly fond of alcohol. This illustration shows members of Black Bart's crew celebrating on the coast of west Africa after a day spent making repairs to their ship.

◀ In this painting by American artist Howard Pyle (1853–1911) a gang of pirates doles out captured loot on a beach. Pirate life was surprisingly democratic. If a captain failed to carry out enough successful raids, he could be voted out of power by the crew.

Female pirates

Life for a European woman at the time of the Golden Age of piracy was generally one of obedience to men. So imagine the scandal when people read tales of female pirates, as bloodthirsty and lawless as their male counterparts! Accounts of the two most famous female pirates of the time, Mary Read and Anne Bonny, became the stuff of legends. It is likely that many other women were involved in pirate life in one way or another, although their lives were never recorded.

▲ Whatever the truth about female pirates, we know that the fate of women captured by pirates was often terrible. Movies usually tone down the historical truth about their treatment. European pirates, for example, thought nothing of torture and murder.

◄ Mary Read was portrayed as a ferocious fighter. She once fought a duel with a pirate who had insulted one of her lovers. The story goes that she ran her cutlass right through her opponent's body.

Women on board

We know that women were completely banned from some pirate ships as part of the pirate code in case they caused fights among the crew. But having females on board a ship during this era was not very unusual. Women occasionally sailed in ordinary ships as wives or mistresses of crew members or as cooks and nurses. We know that women lived on pirate bases, and it is possible that a number of them also went to sea on pirate ships.

Read and Bonny

Mary Read (1690–1720) and Anne Bonny (born c. 1700) sailed the Caribbean alongside a pirate named "Calico" Jack Rackham (died 1720). Disguised as a man, Mary Read had been serving as a British soldier when her ship was captured by Rackham, and she joined his crew. Anne Bonny was already on board, having left her sailor husband to become Rackham's lover. Both women dressed as men and fought alongside the rest of the crew. We know about their exploits from Captain Johnson's book (see page 28) and from the records of their trial.

► While at sea, both Anne Bonny (right) and Mary Read wore men's clothing— a seaman's jacket and canvas pants. They must have been just as strong as their male counterparts in order to carry the cutlass, pistols, and heavy boarding ax shown in this engraving.

▲ People were fascinated by Mary Read and Anne Bonny's story. It inspired many movies that portray a brave female pirate who is able to hold her own in a fight. This is a scene from the 1951 movie *Anne of the Indies*, which was based on the exploits of Anne Bonny.

Trial and death

After taking many prizes, Rackham's ship was captured by the British navy. Only Mary and Anne put up any resistance since the rest of the crew was drunk below deck. All of those captured, including Mary and Anne, were sentenced to hang. The execution of the women was delayed, however, because they were both pregnant. Mary Read soon died of sickness in a Jamaican prison, but it is said that Anne had her child, was given a pardon, and left prison. What happened to her after that is a mystery.

Pirate punishments

The Golden Age of piracy began with warring European countries using pirates to harm their enemies. But when peace returned to Europe in 1714, the seagoing nations made efforts to stamp out piracy because it was harming their growing trade with overseas colonies. Pirates became famous celebrities who attracted large crowds to their trials and executions. By 1730, many of the most notorious pirates and their crews were dead or behind bars. The Golden Age was over.

▲ In 1718 the head of the most famous pirate of all, Blackbeard (see page 23), was cut off and hung on the front of a British navy ship in order to warn others not to aspire to be like him.

Hunting the criminals

British colonial governors called in the navy to help them get rid of troublesome pirates. Woodes Rogers (1679–1732) was a famous pirate hunter of the time. A former privateer, he became the governor of the Bahamas in 1717 and set out with a Royal Navy force to stamp out piracy in a settlement called New Providence. He offered to pardon those pirates who gave up their life of crime, but when they broke their promises, he returned and ordered a mass hanging.

The hempen jig

In England guilty pirates were usually hanged at low tide. Each body was left to be washed by the tide for a day and a half before being cut down and buried in an unmarked grave. The most notorious criminals were covered in tar after their execution and hung in chains in an iron cage to rot as a warning to others not to turn to a life of piracy. Hanging was nicknamed the "hempen jig" because victims seemed to dance on the end of the hemp rope as they jerked in the throes of death.

▶ Pirate punishments were not only handed out by the authorities. A seaman who broke the pirate code could expect no mercy from his captain. For serious offenses, such as running away from a fight, a pirate could be marooned on a remote desert island with little food or fresh water. The chances of survival were slim.

▲ Pirates captured by the authorities were put in chains to stop them from escaping before their trial. These leg shackles (top) and handcuffs (bottom) date from the 1600s.

Strangling and slavery

The French often sent guilty pirates to work in their colonies as slaves. The Spanish chose the garrote (strangling with a cord) as their method of pirate execution, but other grisly on-the-spot punishments were reported from time to time. In one incident, early in the 1600s, the Spanish tied captured pirates to stakes, cut off their limbs, and smeared the stumps with honey. Then they left the unfortunate criminals to be eaten alive by insects.

▶ The famous Scottish pirate Captain William Kidd (1645–1701) was captured, tried for murder, and hanged. His body was displayed in an iron cage at Tilbury Point, on the banks of the Thames river estuary near London, England. The condemned man was measured for his chains before execution, so he knew what his fate would be. Kidd's rotting corpse hung there for years as a gruesome warning to other sailors not to turn to piracy.

▲ Occasionally, pirates had to clean off barnacles and seaweed that built up on a ship's hull and slowed it down. The ship had to be pulled onto a beach for this job—called careening. It was a dangerous time for the pirate crews, so they tried to keep their careening sites a secret. There was no escape if they were caught by a navy patrol with their ship out of the water.

Chinese pirate fleets

From the 1600s–1800s, piracy thrived in the China seas. Along China's vast coastline, countless islands and hidden estuaries made ideal pirate bases. Unlike the pirates of the Caribbean, who tended to work on their own, the Chinese worked in huge, well-organized fleets. They used violent threats to blackmail money from coastal settlements and merchant ships. The piracy business became so important that its leaders ruled over large areas, like mini emperors.

▼ The junk was the all-purpose ship used by both merchant and pirate fleets in the China seas. The basic design was simple, with three masts carrying sails made of bamboo matting. Many pirate junks were trading ships that had been captured and converted. They were armed with cannons and swivel guns called lantaka. The larger junks could carry up to 200 crew and were more than a match for the ships of the Chinese navy.

▲ In 1849 a large pirate fleet led by Chui Apoo (died 1851) was hunted down and destroyed off the coast of China by British naval gunboats. A navy ship can be seen in the center of this painting, with its distinctive, European-style square sails.

Criminal fleets

In the mid-1600s a pirate leader named Cheng Chih Lung (dates unknown) built up a fleet of several hundred ships that controlled most of the Chinese coast. The Chinese emperor, recognizing his power, made him an admiral in the navy—with responsibility for hunting pirates! More than 100 years later, the pirate chief Ching-I (1784–1844) commanded around 30,000 crew in the biggest pirate fleet that ever sailed. His fleet was organized into six squadrons, each with its own area of operation. It was, in effect, a floating criminal army.

A family business

Piracy in the China seas was a family affair. Most pirate captains sailed with their wives and family on board. Pirate leaders employed family members in their businesses, and it was common for relatives to inherit a fleet when a captain died. When Cheng Chih Lung was betrayed and killed by the emperor, his son, Kuo Hsing Yeh (1624–1662), took over his father's fleet. He drove the official naval forces out of his territory and built up a huge trading empire.

Steam-powered pirate hunting

The opium drug trade between China and Europe was very profitable, and the British sent their navy to protect it from piracy. The final showdown came in 1849, when a joint Royal Navy and Chinese force fought the notorious Shap'ng-Tsai (dates unknown) off the coast of Vietnam. The steam-powered British warships were the most formidable in the world. They trapped the pirate fleet and then bombarded and destroyed it. Shap'ng-Tsai escaped, but it was the end of the pirate fleets.

▲ Chinese pirates traditionally fought with a large two-handed sword, while Japanese pirates fought with a smaller sword in each hand. But Western weapons were also used, as shown in this picture of a Japanese pirate chief holding a revolver.

▶ The islands of Indonesia and the Philippines provided a safe refuge for pirates, as they still do today (see pages 52–53). The inlets and islands of Borneo and Sumatra (shown here) sheltered fierce, headhunting pirate tribes.

Political pirates

Although the Golden Age of piracy had ended, the upheavals of the Revolutionary War (1775–1783) and the Napoleonic wars (1799–1815) saw another surge in piracy—this time driven by politics. The American and French navies were not strong enough to take on the British Royal Navy alone, so they hired privateers to harass the British merchant fleet and disrupt trade.

Privateers for independence

In 1775, at the start of the Revolutionary War between Great Britain and its American colonies, the American navy had barely 30 ships. So the Americans hired privateers to attack British merchant vessels. Operating from Atlantic ports, such as Boston, Massachusetts, and Baltimore, Maryland, they devastated British trade to the Americas, seizing almost 3,000 ships. At one time, up to 500 privateers were regularly attacking the British merchant fleet.

▲ This photograph portrays Haiti-born pirate Jean Laffite as a romantic hero in a 1938 movie *The Buccaneer.*

▼ John Paul Jones's greatest feat was the capture of the British 50-gun warship *Serapis* in the North Sea in 1779. Jones's ship, the *Bonhomme Richard*, was a converted merchant vessel. Uncertain of the state of his cannon, he decided to fight the *Serapis* at close range. The battle was so vicious that Jones's own vessel eventually sank—but not before the captain of the severely damaged *Serapis* had surrendered.

Scourge of the British

The Scotsman John Paul Jones (1747–1792) was viewed as a pirate by the British, but he was a hero to the Americans. Working as an officer in the American navy, he sailed to Europe in 1778 in order to attack British ships. France supported the Americans in the Revolutionary War, so Jones was allowed to operate from French Channel ports. He captured merchant vessels and even landed on the coast of northwestern England, destroying ships in the port of Whitehaven.

Pirate or hero?

Jean Laffite (c. 1780–c. 1825) was a pirate who operated on both sides of the law. In the early 1800s he was based in Barataria Bay, south of New Orleans, Louisiana, illegally smuggling and slave trading. His pirate fleet was raided by an American naval force in 1814, but one year later he won a pardon for helping the city of New Orleans defeat a British attempt to capture it. Laffite was a national hero for a while, until he stole a ship and sailed to Texas to continue his life of piracy.

French corsairs

During the Napoleonic wars Great Britain fought France and blockaded the French navy in its home ports. France hit back at the British using privateers called corsairs. They operated from French Channel ports such as St. Malo and Dunkerque, which had been pirate haunts for centuries. They captured up to 2,000 British merchant ships during the early years of the wars. The French corsairs became national heroes and very rich men owing to their raids.

◄ Robert Surcouf (1773–1827), portrayed here in the movie *The Sea Pirate*, was one of the most famous French corsairs of Napoleonic times. He attacked British ships in the Indian Ocean.

Secretive smugglers

Smuggling across the English Channel was common during the 1700s and 1800s. To finance its many wars at the time, the British government demanded the payment of high taxes, called duty, on luxury goods that were imported from abroad such as brandy and tea. The tax demands were so heavy that smuggling developed into a large industry. The smuggled goods—known as contraband—were secretly shipped to remote parts of the British coast in order to avoid paying money to government tax agents, or revenue men.

Nighttime deliveries

Smuggling boats arrived on the English coast in darkness. Gang members on land would signal to the ships when the coast was clear of revenue men. The smugglers would then bring the cargo to shore, and the gang would carry the goods off the beach in order for them to be hidden. Smuggling ships were light and fast, and they had sails that allowed them to move with or against the wind. This was important if they had to come in close to shore and get away quickly to avoid being captured. The boats were usually painted black, with dark sails for nighttime camouflage.

Secret cargoes

The smugglers' most popular goods were brandy, gin, tobacco, tea, and silk and lace for fine clothes. Wealthy British people would buy these luxuries without asking where they came from, and the smugglers' profits were high. Brandy and gin were smuggled in small barrels that could be hidden easily on a ship. Tobacco was packed into small, waterproof bundles. In an emergency the tobacco would be thrown overboard into the sea. Because they floated, the bundles could be picked up later by gang members in rowboats.

◀ In this dramatic illustration smugglers are being attacked by revenue men (in blue jackets). Many violent battles were fought between the two groups. Smugglers fought hard to escape capture and punishment.

Smuggling killers

Whole communities were involved in smuggling since it took many people to land and hide contraband. It was also safer that way. If all of the locals profited from the trade, they were more likely to stay quiet about it. Some smuggling gangs used violent threats to ensure silence. The most notorious was the Hawkhurst gang, which operated on the Romney marshes of southeastern England. Seven of its leaders were hanged in 1749 after the torture and murder of a customs official and a shoemaker. The official was buried alive, and the shoemaker was thrown into a well.

▲ In this advertisement from 1891 smugglers are taking a barrel of smuggled whiskey to a deserted beach. They are shown as cheerful, harmless men, but in reality smugglers were often violent and dangerous criminals.

▼ After the mid-1700s captured British smugglers were usually hanged only if they had murdered someone. Otherwise many were transported. This meant that they were sent to British colonies overseas, such as Australia, to work as slaves. While they waited to sail, prisoners were sometimes kept in prison hulks—rotting, stinking old ships that were anchored close to shore. This painting from 1828 shows a prison hulk in Portsmouth harbor, on the south coast of England.

Smuggling facts and fiction

The English Channel is the setting for smuggling legends that date back to the 1700s. Many of the stories tell about how the smugglers tried to trick the authorities in order to avoid being captured. As with piracy, these smuggling stories have fueled the imaginations of writers and moviemakers. Romantic myths have developed around secret tunnels, murderous wreckers, and aristocratic criminal masterminds.

▲ Smugglers regularly crisscrossed the English Channel carrying a wide variety of goods. The French emperor Napoleon I (1769–1821) had supplies of gold smuggled from England in order to finance his wars.

Hiding the stash

Smugglers used many clever tricks to hide contraband. Tobacco was woven into rope and piled innocently on deck. Brandy and gin were smuggled in secret compartments that were built into the bottoms of ordinary water barrels. When revenue men began to measure the depth of the barrels, the smugglers built special compartments so that the sides of the barrels held the liquor, while the barrel depths appeared normal.

Pits were sometimes dug at the top of a beach to hide a smuggled shipment until it could be moved out. These pits had to be very deep because revenue men poked long probes into the sand to look for contraband. Specially built smuggling tunnels were much more rare, but there is an example in Hayle in southwestern England. It runs for several hundred feet from the coast to the town.

▼ According to legend, villagers living on the coast of Cornwall would steal the washed-up cargoes of ships that had been wrecked in storms. It was even rumored that surviving crew members would be murdered and their valuables stolen.

Cunning criminals

Smugglers made careful plans in order to land a cargo. Often, if the coast was not clear, the smuggling ship would sail to one of several alternative landing points. Smugglers built coastal houses with special towers or high windows from which a prearranged light signal could be sent. They also made lanterns that concentrated the light in a beam out to sea but not to the surrounding countryside.

Master smugglers

Smugglers needed financial assistance because it was expensive to buy the cargo overseas. Shadowy figures financed the illegal trade and made fortunes, especially in southeastern England, close to the London markets. As with the illegal drug trade today, they were rarely identified or arrested. It was the people who actually carried out the smuggling who were caught and punished.

▶ Many of Cornwall's smuggling tales feature wreckers—villagers who deliberately wrecked ships close to the shore. They lit beacons to fool a vessel's crew into thinking that they were close to port when, in fact, they were being guided onto rocks.

SUMMARY OF CHAPTER 2: THE GOLDEN AGE

A ship's cannon dating from the Golden Age

Pirates, smugglers, and politics

The Golden Age of piracy lasted for only 40 years, roughly from 1690 to 1730. As Europe became more peaceful at the end of the 1600s, rulers no longer needed their privateer forces—but the pirates continued to attack cargo ships because the profits were so high. But now the pirates were harming the trade of the governments that they once aided, so they were hunted down and punished.

Smuggling in the Golden Age was political, too. It was a way of avoiding the heavy tax that governments placed on imported goods in order to help pay for their wars.

The legend of the Golden Age pirates

Writers turned the pirates of the Golden Age into antiheroes—evil but fascinating characters. They based their stories on the reports of eyewitnesses who told of the extraordinary adventures and wicked cruelties of men such as Blackbeard, Henry Morgan, and William Kidd. We cannot tell how true some of the writings are, but we do know that colorful reports of pirate lives and deaths sold well and were the inspiration for many vivid pirate legends.

The truth

In reality, pirates of the 1600s and 1700s were criminals who murdered innocent people at sea and terrorized communities on land. Smugglers of the time could also be very violent, using threats and even torture to silence people who witnessed their crimes.

In addition, the Golden Age buccaneers and pirates helped start the slave trade that forced millions of Africans to work against their will in the Americas. But there is no doubt that they also led extraordinary lives that will continue to fascinate us for centuries to come.

Go further . . .

The Pirate's Realm is packed with fascinating information, games, and a list of all of the pirate museums around the world, with links: www.thepiratesrealm.com

Read *Treasure Island*, the classic pirate adventure, written by Robert Louis Stevenson (Signet Classics). *Moonfleet* is an action-packed smuggling tale by John Meade Falkner (Penguin).

Pirates! by Celia Rees (Bloomsbury, 2005)

The World of Ships by Philip Wilkinson (Kingfisher, 2005)

Eyewitness Books: Pirate by Richard Platt (Dorling Kindersley, 2007)

Historian
Reads and writes about people, places, and events from the past.

Prop and costume maker
Creates historical costumes and artifacts, often for use in movies and television programs.

Researcher
Studies a specific area of history, looking at old documents and accounts for historical clues. May also advise makers of movies and TV programs.

Screenwriter
Writes the script for a movie, including all of the actors' lines and the action scenes.

Cornwall, in the far southwest of England, has many smuggling coves and inns. You can also visit the National Maritime Museum in Cornwall: Discovery Quay, Falmouth TR11 3QY, U.K. Phone: +44 (0) 1326 313388 www.nmmc.co.uk

The east coast of the U.S. is dotted with maritime museums. These include the following:

The New England Pirate Museum 274 Derby Street, Salem, MA 01970 www.piratemuseum.com

The Mel Fisher Maritime Heritage Museum 200 Greene Street, Key West, FL 33040 www.melfisher.org

Refugees, such as these Vietnamese people, often fall victim to modern-day pirates and smugglers (see pages 50–51).

CHAPTER 3

Modern piracy and smuggling

Piracy and smuggling are not simply crimes from past centuries. They are flourishing today and are often organized by vicious international crime gangs such as the Mafia and the Chinese Triads.

Piracy grows year by year, especially around Nigeria and parts of Southeast Asia. Today's pirates have fast boats, high-tech

equipment, and machine guns. They prey on merchant ships and yachts, stealing from the crews and sometimes even capturing an entire ship and its cargo.

Smuggling is a major modern crime too. Drugs, people, and wildlife have replaced alcohol and tobacco as the main goods in this illegal activity.

Rumrunners

In the 1920s alcohol was made illegal in the United States. This era was known as Prohibition, and it caused a sharp rise in alcohol smuggling by sea. Illegal shipments of rum and whiskey were landed along the Atlantic and Pacific coasts of the U.S. and then transported to big cities for secret sales. The smugglers were nicknamed "rumrunners." It was a very profitable trade that attracted violent gangsters such as Al Capone.

▲ This 1921 magazine illustration shows American authorities destroying smuggled alcohol by pouring it down a drain. The police might have captured some of it by raiding illegal bars called speakeasies.

Rum row

Fleets of large vessels weighed down with alcohol would sail toward the U.S. but anchor perfectly legally outside the 3-mi. (5-km) territorial limit around the coast. Smaller boats would sail out to them, load up with cargo, and smuggle it back to the coast. A line of big ships anchored at sea was called a rum row, and this could mean up to 14 vessels. At first, riotous parties were held on the rum-row ships. People sailed or even rowed out to them from the shore for a drunken night out, as well as for smuggling. Later the territorial limit was changed to 12 mi. (19km) out from the shore, and rumrunning became much more difficult.

Gangsters get involved

Prohibition was unpopular, and many Americans were prepared to buy alcohol secretly—so the smugglers made a lot of money. At first, the rum-runners were a mixed group of sailors and fishermen, but then gangster mobs took over. They drove ordinary boatmen from the trade with threats, violence, and even murder. Rumrunning became a deadly chase between coast-guard boats and gangster vessels, both armed with deck-mounted machine guns.

◄ These torpedoes, which are full of alcohol, were confiscated from a rum-row schooner (a small, fast sailing ship). They were designed to be shot from the schooner, collected, and then dragged to shore by smaller boats. Smuggling alcohol during Prohibition was known as bootlegging.

Tricks of the trade

Rumrunning boats often had false bottoms to hide alcohol. On fishing boats a layer of fish might cover up the real cargo, and one rumrunner even designed a vehicle that he could load with alcohol and tow behind his boat to look like fishing equipment. The gangsters built fast, armor-plated boats to outrun the coast guard, with the powerful engines muffled to be as quiet as possible. Sometimes they installed devices that poured oily smoke into the path of a coast-guard boat on the chase.

▶ The notorious American gangster Al Capone (1899–1947) was involved in rumrunning. He was a "mobster"—the leader of a violent organized-crime gang that ran many illegal businesses. The mobsters made big profits from alcohol smuggling. The law breaking became so bad that Prohibition was ended in 1933.

▼ Prohibition law-enforcement agents examine confiscated cases of whiskey on board a coast-guard ship. Boat chases often took place on foggy nights, when the smugglers tried to land their goods unseen.

Modern-day smuggling

Oceangoing smuggling still takes place around the world. Smugglers make big profits by avoiding government taxes on imported goods, by bringing in illegal cargo, such as drugs, and by smuggling people between countries. Heavily armed and violent gangs are often involved, as they have been for centuries.

▲ In 2001 British port police found the drug heroin hidden inside thousands of individual almond nuts. The drugs, worth $7.5 million, had been shipped from Sri Lanka.

Deadly cargoes

Tobacco and alcohol are still smuggled by sea to avoid paying duty, or import tax, to governments—just as they were hundreds of years ago. Today, however, larger profits are made from smuggling drugs and arms (weapons). Innocent-looking yachts may conceal cargoes of cocaine or heroin to be sold for high prices on city streets. Arms are illegally smuggled to war zones or for use by criminals.

Speedy smugglers

Today smugglers use lightweight "go fast" boats to get their cargo to shore. These are usually equipped with several engines so that they can reach top speeds in a chase. Because the boats are built with no metallic parts, they cannot be detected by radar except at close range or in a calm sea. The best way for coast guards to catch "go fast" boats is to spot them from above, by helicopter.

Smuggling hot spots

The world's largest drug producers are found in South America and Asia, but the major drug markets are in North America and Europe (see map below). To move the drugs from one country to another involves smuggling them undetected across borders, often through ports or marinas. The Gulf of Mexico is a smuggling hot spot, just as it was in the days of Jean Laffite (see page 37). Drugs and arms are brought by sea from Central America through the Gulf of Mexico to isolated spots on the southern U.S. coast.

A violent crime

Modern smuggling often involves violence. Criminals double-cross one another, use threats to scare people into keeping quiet, and are heavily armed in order to resist arrest. The penalties for drug smuggling are high. In some countries the automatic punishment is death.

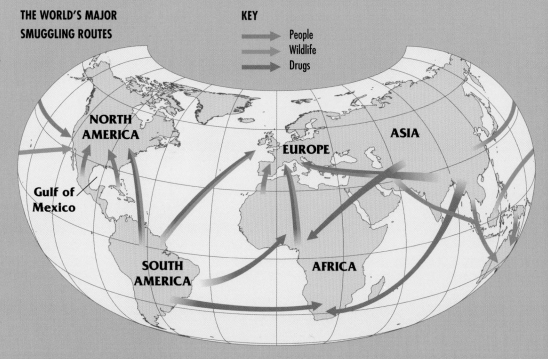

THE WORLD'S MAJOR SMUGGLING ROUTES

KEY
People
Wildlife
Drugs

NORTH AMERICA

Gulf of Mexico

SOUTH AMERICA

EUROPE

ASIA

AFRICA

▶ Customs officials use fast, inflatable boats, called RHIs (rigid-hulled inflatables), to chase after drug-smuggling vessels. The lightweight RHIs can reach a top speed of up to 55 mph (90km/h). They are equipped with radar and, in some countries, several types of weapons.

Wildlife smugglers

Wildlife is now the third-most-profitable smuggling cargo after drugs and arms. The Worldwide Fund for Nature estimates that criminal gangs could be making profits of up to an astounding $20 billion each year from smuggling live animals and rare plants to unprincipled collectors. The criminals do not care about bringing rare creatures close to extinction or causing them terrible suffering on their illegal journeys.

Smuggling from South America

Up to 11 million animals per year are smuggled from South America, mostly to the U.S., where they are sold illegally to collectors over the Internet or through corrupt dealers. Many highly endangered animals are under threat from smugglers, including rare parrots, monkeys, and snakes. But, out of every ten animals captured for smuggling, it is estimated that only one survives the journey to become an exotic pet.

▶ The rare and beautiful red-tailed black cockatoo is a type of parrot. It is protected by law in Australia, but some collectors pay up to $25,000 for one smuggled specimen.

◀ These macaque monkeys are chained up for sale in an Asian market. Some kidnapped animals are lucky enough to be rescued from markets and returned to the wild, but most die in captivity.

Big profits from cruelty

Rare animals that survive smuggling make bigger profits for criminals than smuggled drugs. An Amazonian blue macaw might sell for $25,000, for example, and an endangered tamarin monkey can net $20,000. Gangs have been known to combine both trades by hiding drugs inside rare animals. In one example smuggled snakes from Colombia were forced to swallow cocaine-filled bags. Customs officials discovered the snakes and noticed the unusual bulges inside them. Sadly, many of the snakes died from swallowing the drugs.

The fight against smugglers

Rare animals are often transported by boats through busy ports, where it is difficult for the authorities to check every cargo. The police try to track the movements of smuggling gangs by talking to local contacts and searching street markets where illegally captured animals are sold. They also investigate pet dealers and Web sites to find out who is buying the animals.

From orchids to ivory

Modern smugglers make money from all types of goods. Rare orchids are illegally dug up and smuggled from countries such as New Zealand and Peru. Caviar (fish eggs), one of the world's most expensive foods, is smuggled from Russia. Rare tigers are illegally killed, and their body parts are sold in Asia as ingredients in traditional medicines. Elephants and rhinoceros are killed for their ivory tusks, which are used in medicines and carvings.

▶ Rare orchids have been prized by collectors for their exotic beauty since the 1800s. There are more than 25,000 different types of orchids. This is a lady's slipper, one of the most commonly smuggled types.

◀ Reptiles and insects make big profits for smugglers. Chameleons, such as this panther chameleon from the African island of Madagascar, are illegally caught and sold to collectors as pets.

Smuggling people

People smuggling is growing rapidly around the world. Organized criminal gangs smuggle large numbers of people illegally across country borders by boat, truck, or plane. They make big profits by charging for the dangerous trip and also by threatening or blackmailing their clients.

Dangerous journey

People who move from one country to another are known as migrants. Smuggled migrants face a hazardous journey. The smugglers cram hundreds of people onto dirty, unsafe boats, often without enough food. The crews may be violent and sometimes throw sick people into the sea. In some areas of Southeast Asia the smugglers' boats even run the risk of being attacked by murderous pirates.

Why people pay

In some countries many poor people are willing to pay all of the money they have to criminal gangs that will smuggle them across the border. Their destinations are wealthier nations, such as Great Britain, Australia, and the U.S., where they can start new lives. They may want to work in a country where wages are higher or escape violence, war, or political oppression in their own lands.

Threats and blackmail

Once people have been transported illegally into a country, they are often threatened by the smugglers and forced to work for criminals, passing on their earnings and taking part in crimes themselves. If they refuse, they may be killed or their relatives back home may be threatened with violence. The smuggled people find themselves in a trap, unable to tell the police what is happening to them.

▲ In the late 1990s a war in the Balkan region of Europe led to thousands of refugees flooding into other European countries. These people are fleeing from Kosovo to Albania. Wars often lead to a rise in people smuggling as refugees try to find better lives elsewhere.

▼ A U.S. Coast Guard vessel intercepts a boat packed with illegal migrants from the Caribbean country of Haiti. Most of them will have paid criminals to get them onto the boat, in the hope of starting new lives in the U.S.

Risking everything

One of the world's people-smuggling hot spots is the Strait of Gibraltar. This narrow strip of sea, between Morocco and Spain, separates Africa and Europe by only 8 mi. (13km). Migrants squeeze onto small, overcrowded boats to make the crossing. People who fall overboard often drown in the dangerous, fast-flowing currents. Another busy smuggling route runs from China to Europe. Migrants pay Chinese gangs to cram them into trucks or even ship containers for long and often fatal journeys.

▶ An illegal migrant held by police in Tarifa, a town facing Morocco on the coast of southern Spain. Migrants regularly land there by boat, often brought across the Strait of Gibraltar by criminal gangs.

Pirates today

Piracy did not die out during the time of Blackbeard. Today it is a growing crime that is increasingly well organized and violent. Heavily armed pirates attack merchant ships and yachts in fast boats, terrorizing the crews or murdering them and then stealing what they can. Piracy is a particular problem in Indonesia, Bangladesh, Vietnam, India, Nigeria, and the ports and rivers of Brazil.

▼ These Filipino pirates are using a flat-bottomed canoe that can move fast and is also useful in shallow water. They are armed with powerful rifles. In 2006 15 sailors were reported to have been killed by pirates worldwide. Many more deaths may go unreported.

◄ Isolated coastal villages in places such as the Philippines sometimes shelter pirate gangs that threaten passing vessels.

Dangerous waters
The Strait of Malacca—a narrow strip of water between Indonesia, Singapore, and Malaysia—is said to be the world's most dangerous shipping route. There are rich pickings for pirate gangs that hide among the many islands. More than one fourth of the world's cargo ships pass through the strait every year, including many oil tankers. These tankers and other large merchant ships have small crews that are easily overpowered by swarms of armed gunmen.

Speedy attacks

Modern pirates tend to hide in inlets and on islands. They speed out to surprise their prey, disguised in masks and armed with automatic rifles. They may steal from local fishermen or yachts or attack larger merchant ships to steal the cargo and valuables on board. Occasionally, they take over a ship and demand a ransom for the safe return of the crew.

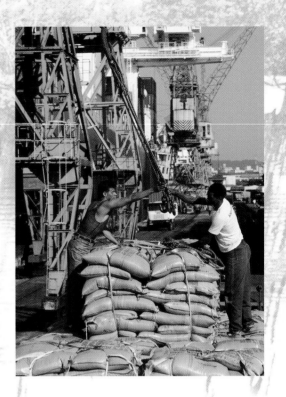

▲ Major ports are hotbeds of smuggling and piracy. The ports of Brazil, such as Santos (above), are among the most dangerous in the world, along with the ports of Indonesia and Bangladesh. Every month millions of dollars worth of illegal goods and stolen cargo are smuggled through these ports, with the help of corrupt officials.

Piracy and corruption

Sophisticated gangs use high-tech methods to steal from merchant ships in the Strait of Malacca. They plan raids on specific cargoes, using inside information from corrupt office workers in shipping companies. They intercept e-mails and telephone calls to find out what the cargoes are, how many crew members a ship is carrying, and what the route will be. Dishonest government officials help the gangs hide their crime and sell the stolen cargo.

Amazon attack

In 2001 river piracy hit the headlines when the famous yachtsman Sir Peter Blake (1948–2001) was killed by bandits who raided his boat on the Amazon river in Brazil.

Catching the criminals

Coast-guard crews and port police are at the front line of law enforcement, trying to catch smugglers both in ports and out at sea. They use well-equipped boats and surveillance planes for this dangerous job. On an average day U.S. coast guards search up to 140 vessels and seize narcotics (drugs) worth around $10.8 million.

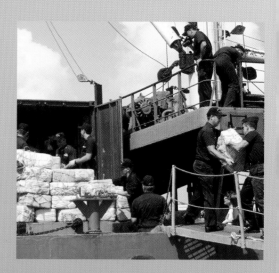

▲ Narcotics worth billions of dollars are smuggled into the U.S. every year. Many of these illegal drugs are hidden in ships and brought into the country through ports. This means that the port police have to be on the lookout for suspect shipments at all times. In this 2003 drug bust in Miami, Florida, police found a huge supply.

▲ Port police use night-vision equipment to see smugglers in the dark. This works either by thermal imaging (which shows the heat given off by objects and people) or by image enhancement (which strengthens small amounts of light so that the image can be seen more clearly). In this image-enhanced picture a suspect holding a briefcase is picked up by night-vision equipment as he crosses a parking lot.

Dangerous work

Coast-guard policing can be a very risky business. In the past smugglers often fought government officials, sometimes even murdering them. Today the danger is still high, so coast-guard police are well trained to deal with armed criminals who resist arrest. Effective police work relies on information. This may come from law-enforcement officers who work undercover to find out about criminal gangs and illegal shipments.

Port searches

If customs officials suspect that a ship docked in port is carrying illegally smuggled cargo, they will search it using a range of equipment. They might use sniffer dogs trained to find drugs or screen the boat with radiation and explosive detectors. To find stowaway migrants, they use devices that measure the level of carbon dioxide gas in cargo containers. If the level is high, it could be a sign that people are inside—because humans breathe out carbon dioxide.

Customs cutters
Coast guards use cutters (boats that are more than 66 ft./20m long) for coastal patrols. On board, there is often a smaller boat such as an RHI (see page 47), which the customs officials use to approach and board any vessel that they want to search. The cutters are often equipped with powerful computers for tracking and navigation, as well as surface radar and other high-tech equipment, in order to pinpoint vessels at sea.

Police to the rescue
In addition to fast boats, coast-guard police use surveillance planes and helicopters to help them find boats at sea. Small vessels full of illegal migrants can most easily be seen from above. These boats are usually unsafe and dangerously overcrowded and may get into trouble. The migrants' only chance of survival might be for a coast-guard plane to spot their boat and attempt a rescue operation.

▲ Rescue helicopters are called out by the coast guard if a boat carrying illegal migrants gets into trouble. Coast guards also have their own spotter helicopters. In some countries these have armed officers on board, who are ready to shoot at the engines of suspicious-looking boats, putting them out of action.

▼ Sniffer dogs can detect drugs ten times faster than humans are able to. Some dogs are cross-trained—this means that they can detect hidden people as well as drugs. In this picture the face of the dog handler has been blurred in order to protect her identity from smugglers.

Shipwreck hunters

Underwater archaeologists study shipwrecks in order to find clues about the people who once lived on board. Some wrecks also contain valuable treasures that can be sold at auctions, and this is why many underwater treasure hunters get involved in wreck hunting. In recent years, as underwater technology has become more sophisticated, some exciting discoveries have been made on sunken pirate ships.

Locating a shipwreck

It is not easy to find a wrecked ship. Researchers spend many hours in libraries and archives, where old documents and records are kept. They read historical letters, journals, and maps to spot clues that point to the area where a ship sank. However, a wreck might be buried or broken up and spread over a wide area. To track down the exact location, wreck hunters use special equipment to carry out a survey. For example, the sea floor can be mapped using magnetometers, which detect metal objects, and sonar equipment, which locates shapes on the seabed.

▲ A ship's logbook (background image) can be a valuable tool to wreck hunters. This example dates from 1790.

▼ These divers are at work in waters off the Bahamas, in the Caribbean. They are using an air-filled balloon to raise a heavy iron cannon from the 17th-century Spanish ship *Nuestra Señora de las Maravillas* to the surface.

► Once the remains of a ship have been pinpointed, divers begin the painstaking job of measuring, mapping, sketching, and taking photographs of the wreck.

Protecting the wreck

The people who discover a wreck usually have salvage rights over it, which means that they can claim what they find. But illegal wreck hunters often arrive to raid a site of its treasures, and in doing so they may damage valuable historical evidence. This is why wreck hunters try to keep a site secret for as long as possible.

Finding objects

First a survey is made of the wreck site. It is important to record exactly where objects are found because this might help archaeologists decide how items were used and who owned them. Divers then use metal detectors, probes, and their hands to make finds. Often they clear away mud and sand using pipes that suck up the dirt like a vacuum cleaner.

Discoveries are lifted up very carefully to the surface. Objects brought up from the seabed rot rapidly in fresh air. They must be kept wet, or they will crumble before they can be preserved.

◄ These underwater archaeologists are examining a stash of Spanish coins that they have just recovered from the wreck of the pirate ship *Whydah*, off the coast of Cape Cod.

▲ This shoe was recovered from the pirate ship *Whydah*, which was captained by Samuel "Black Sam" Bellamy (died 1717). Divers also found a human leg bone that was still clothed in a silk stocking.

▶ If a wreck lies in very deep water, scuba divers are unable to swim down to it. Instead submersibles are sent to explore the remains. A famous example of this is the *Titanic*, which sank in the Atlantic Ocean in 1912. It lies at a depth of around 2.5 mi. (4km), and only a few manned submersibles can reach it. This is the Russian submersible *Mir I*, just after a trip down to the *Titanic*.

Patient preservation

Preservation and restoration work on the finds from a wreck can take many years and a lot of patience. Wood has to be washed over and over again in order to get rid of the sea salt. Then it is soaked in chemicals to stop it from rotting, and barnacles are gently removed. Metal objects corrode (rot away) under water, but on land this crumbling can be stopped by putting the find in a tank of water and passing an electrical current through it.

Fine dressers

The first-ever pirate shipwreck to be found and explored was the *Whydah*, which sank off the coast of Cape Cod during a howling storm in 1717. The finds included thousands of coins as well as personal items that tell us a lot about the pirates who lived on board. For example, belt buckles, buttons, and jewelry suggest that the crew liked to dress well.

All washed up

Since the wreck of the *Whydah* was discovered in 1984, more exciting pirate-ship finds have been made. Wreck hunters have located vessels off the U.S. coast that belonged to Captain Morgan and Blackbeard. In 1996 a wreck thought to be a Barbary pirate ship was discovered after some Arab coins were washed up on a beach in Salcombe Bay in southern England. Maybe the pirates were on their way to raid the coast for slaves.

◀ This stash of treasure, now kept in the British Museum in London, England, was recovered by divers from the seabed in Salcombe Bay. In total, the collection includes more than 400 gold coins, broken pieces of gold jewelry, pottery shards, and a merchant's seal. No one knows the identity of the ship that carried the treasure, but it may have been a Barbary pirate vessel.

SUMMARY OF CHAPTER 3: MODERN PIRACY AND SMUGGLING

From local to international
In the past smuggling was carried out by local gangs as a way of cheating the government out of import taxes. In contrast, modern smugglers are highly organized criminals who have contacts around the world. Law-enforcement agencies work internationally, too, cooperating to try to stop the harm that these crimes cause. The smuggling of people, drugs, and wildlife involves cruelty and misery on a much larger scale than ever before.

Today's pirates may be local fishermen who boost their incomes by stealing valuable goods, or they may be criminal gangs that are trying to make big profits quickly.

High-tech crime
Modern pirates and smugglers have high-tech equipment such as night-vision goggles and satellite-navigation systems. They use the latest weapons and high-speed boats. The crime-busting authorities have to be just as well equipped to have any chance of catching the criminals. Governments spend large amounts of money on coast-guard patrols and vessel searches.

High-tech discoveries
Underwater archaeologists are using newly developed high-tech equipment to make exciting discoveries. They are bringing shipwreck stories to life by raising to the surface objects that have been lost for centuries on the seabed. Their fascinating finds tell us a great deal about the hazardous and often brutal lives of the pirates and smugglers of the past.

A small submarine used by Colombian drug smugglers in the 1990s

Go further . . .

Meet the crew of the *Whydah*—including Captain Samuel Bellamy and ship surgeon Dr. James Ferguson— and learn about their lives at sea and their untimely deaths: www.nationalgeographic.com/whydah/main.html

To go piracy and shipwreck Web surfing, visit: kids.yahoo.com. Then type in "shipwrecks" or "pirates" to get a long list of fun, kid-friendly sites to check out.

Discover more about endangered species of animals and plants on the Red List database: www.iucnredlist.org

Coast-guard officer
Monitors the movements of ships and may be involved in sea rescues.

Customs official
Fights illegal smuggling by searching people, vehicles, and cargoes at ports and airports.

Diver
Trains to dive safely in the ocean, possibly to work on historical wrecks.

Lifeboat crew member
Volunteer who comes to the aid of ships that are in trouble at sea.

Oceanographer
Studies the oceans of the world, including wildlife and the seabed.

Objects from the wreck of the *Whydah* are on display at the Expedition *Whydah* Sea Lab and Learning Center: Macmillan Wharf, Provincetown, MA 02657 www.whydah.com

To find out the location and Web site address of your closest maritime museum, go to: www.maritimemuseums.net

Visit the British Museum to see coins, jewelry, and pottery recovered from the Salcombe Bay wreck site:
Great Russell Street
London WC1B 3DG, U.K.
Phone: +44 (0) 20 7323 8299
www.thebritishmuseum.org

Glossary

◄ ► Two ships do battle at close range in the 1995 pirate movie *Cutthroat Island*.

aft Toward the back (stern) of a ship.

antiseptic A substance that kills germs and prevents infections.

arms Weapons.

barbarian An uncivilized and violent person.

Barbary pirate A Muslim pirate from the coast of north Africa.

bowsprit A long mast sticking out from the front of a sailing ship.

buccaneer A pirate who attacked Spanish ships in the Americas during the 1600s.

careening Cleaning the barnacles off a ship's hull.

cargo The goods being carried by a ship.

city-state A political system in which an independent city rules over the surrounding countryside. Ancient Greece was made up of many city-states.

coast guard Coastline police and rescue services.

colony Land claimed and settled by another country.

contraband Smuggled goods.

corsair A French word for a privateer or pirate. Also the name given to a Barbary pirate.

cutlass A short sword with a wide blade.

doubloon A Spanish gold coin.

duty A government tax on luxury goods, such as tobacco, brought into a country from overseas.

fore Toward the front of a ship.

forecastle A raised deck at the front of a ship.

galleon A large, slow, and sturdy treasure ship, used by the Spanish from the 1500s to the 1700s.

galley A boat powered by both sails and rows of oarsmen.

"go fast" boat A small, fast, modern boat. It has a lightweight, V-shaped hull made from fiberglass.

Golden Age The period roughly between 1690 and 1730 when piracy was common off the coast of the Americas and in the Indian Ocean.

harem A group of wives kept by a Muslim ruler.

hempen jig The nickname pirates gave to hanging.

hulk An old ship used as a prison.

hull The outer shell of a ship.

import To buy or bring in goods from another country.

Jolly Roger A flag used by pirates to signal an attack.

junk An Asian ship with sails made out of bamboo matting.

keel A ship's lowest timber, running the full length of the vessel and supporting the entire frame of the hull.

Knights of St. John A band of Christian knights, formed in the early 1100s.

lateen sail A triangular sail, used on Arab boats.

letter of marque A license given to a sailor, granting him or her permission to attack enemy ships. *See also* privateer.

magnetometer An instrument that measures the magnetic field of an object. It can be used under water to detect metal objects buried below the seabed.

merchant ship A ship carrying cargo to sell.

migrant A person who moves from one country to another.

musket An early type of gun with a long barrel.

Muslim A person who follows the religion of Islam.

mutiny A rebellion against authority. In a mutiny at sea ordinary sailors would take over the ship from their captain.

narcotics Drugs.

opium A drug made from the seeds of the poppy flower.

Ottoman Empire The Turkish empire in Europe, Africa, and Asia that lasted from the 1200s to 1923.

piece of eight A Spanish silver coin.

piracy Robbery at sea, stealing or destroying ships, and raiding settlements along a coast.

pirate code A list of rules that pirate crews agreed to obey.

pirate round A voyage from the Americas to west Africa and the Indian Ocean and back again.

political oppression The bad treatment of someone because of his or her political beliefs.

poop deck A raised deck at the back of a ship.

privateer A sailor given a license by a country's government to attack the ships of an enemy.

prize A ship stolen by a pirate.

Prohibition A law banning the sale of alcohol in the U.S. during the 1920s. It led to smuggling.

radar A system for tracking objects using radio signals.

ransom A fee demanded for the release of a captured person.

rapier A long, narrow, two-edged sword, popular in the 1500s and 1600s.

refugee A person who has escaped from danger or a problem, often by moving from one country to another.

revenue men British tax officials.

rigging The network of ropes that help hold up a ship's masts and that allow the sails to be controlled.

rudder A large, flat structure attached by hinges to the rear of a ship and turned to steer the vessel.

rumrunner Someone who smuggled alcohol into the U.S. during the years of Prohibition.

scurvy A disease of the skin and gums caused by a lack of vitamin C in a person's diet. It can be prevented by eating citrus fruits.

sloop A small, fast ship with one mast and a triangular sail.

smuggler A person who breaks the law by transporting goods or people secretly from one country to another.

sonar A system that uses sound signals to measure the depth of an object in water.

Spanish Main The Spanish colonies of the Caribbean, Central America, and the shores of South America.

stern The rear of a ship.

transportation A punishment in which criminals were sent to a faraway colony as slaves.

Viking One of the Scandinavian warriors who invaded Europe from the 700s–1000s.

weevil A type of beetle.

Index

Acknowledgments

The publisher would like to thank the following for permission to reproduce their material. Every care has been taken to trace copyright holders. However, if there have been unintentional omissions or failure to trace copyright holders, we apologize and will, if informed, endeavor to make corrections in any future edition.

Key: *b* = bottom, *c* = center, *l* = left, *r* = right, *t* = top

Cover/Corbis/Joel W. Rogers; cover *c* Corbis/Archivo Iconografico, S.A.; cover *r* Getty Hulton; page 1 Mary Evans Picture Library; 2–3 *The Buccaneers,* by Frederick Judd Waugh (1861–1940)/Private Collection/www.bridgeman.co.uk; 4–5 Corbis/Michael S. Yamashita; 7*b* akg-images/Gilles Mermet; 8*bl* Ancient Art and Architecture Collection Ltd.; 8–9*tc* akg-images/Erich Lessing; 11*br* akg-images; 12*tr* Corbis/Christie's Images; 12*bl* The Art Archive; 12–13*b* National Maritime Museum, London; 14*bl* Ancient Art & Architecture Collection Ltd.; 15*tr* Mary Evans Picture Library; 14–15*b* Corbis/ Bettmann; 16*tl* Corbis/Richard T. Nowitz; 16–17 Mary Evans Picture Library; 17*tl* The Art Archive/Museo Regional de Oaxaca Mexico/Dagli Orti; 17*tr* Mary Evans Picture Library; 18*tl* akg-images/British Library; 19*t* Rex/Percy Hatchman; 20*bl* Mary Evans Picture Library; 20*tr* Heritage-Images/The British Library; 21 Mary Evans Picture Library; 22*bl* Tina Chambers © Dorling Kindersley; 23*br* Hulton Archive/Getty Images; 24*tr* Corbis/Bettmann; 24*bl* Rex/C. W. Disney/Everett (EVT); 25*b* Corbis/Bettmann; 27*tr* akg-images; 27*br* Still Pictures/Benny Odeur; 28–29*b* Mary Evans Picture Library; 29*tr* Corbis/The Mariners' Museum; 28*tr* Topfoto/British Museum/HIP; 30*bl* Corbis/Bettmann; 30*tr* akg-images/Touchstone Pictures/Album; 31*cl* akg-images; 31*r* Corbis; 32–33*b* Howard Pyle, *Marooned,* 1909, Oil on canvas, Delaware Art Museum DAM #1912-936; 32*tl* National Maritime Museum, London; 32*br* akg-images; 32*cr* Heritage-Images/The Board of Trustees of the Armories; 33*cl* The Art Archive/Galleria Estense, Modena/Dagli Orti; 33*r* The Art Archive; 34–35 National Maritime Museum, London; 35*tr* Corbis/Asian Art & Archaeology, Inc.; 35*br* Corbis/Stapleton Collection; 36–37*b* The Art Archive/ Chateau de Blerancourt/Dagli Orti; 36*tr* Corbis/John Springer Collection; 37*br* akg-images/Arco Films/Balcazar Prod./Edic/ Rialto Films/Album; 38*bl* National Maritime Museum, London; 39*tl* Heritage-Images/The National Archives; 39*b* Topfoto; 40*tl* akg-images; 40–41*b* akg-images; 41*tr* Mary Evans Picture Library; 42*tl* Alamy/Doug Steley; 43*t* Corbis/Peter Turnley; 44*tr* Mary Evans Picture Library; 44*bl* Corbis/Bettmann; 45*tr* Corbis/Bettmann; 45*b* Corbis; 46*tl* Topfoto/PA; 47 Topfoto/PA; 48*tr* Corbis/Martin Harvey; 48*bl* Corbis/Robert Maass; 49*tr* Topfoto/Imageworks; 49*br* Corbis/Kevin Schafer; 50*b* Corbis Sygma/Fort Lauderdale Sen; 50*cr* Rex/Sipa Press (SIPA); 51 Corbis/Reuters; 52*cl* Corbis/Albrecht G. Schaefer; 52–53*c* Moreau Jean-Luc/Gamma/Katz; 53*tr* Corbis/Ricardo Azoury; 54*bl* Alamy/3C Stock; 54*tr* Topfoto/Imageworks; 55*tr* Alamy/ Iain Davidson Photographic; 55*br* Rex/Lewis Durham; 56*t* Topfoto/Public Records Office/HIP; 56*b* Corbis/Jeffrey L. Rotman; 56–57 *(background)* Topfoto/Public Records Office/HIP; 57*r* Alamy/Fabrice Bettex; 57*bl* Corbis/Richard T. Nowitz; 58*tl* Getty Images/Time Life Pictures; 58*tr* Corbis/Ralph White; 58*bl* Heritage Images/The British Museum; 59*cr* Corbis/Rob Howard; 60*l* akg-images/Cutthroat Productions/David James/Album; 61*r* akg-images/Cutthroat Productions/David James/Album; 62–63 *(background)* Ancient Art & Architecture Collection Ltd.; 64*b* Mary Evans Picture Library

The publisher would like to thank the following illustrators:
Steve Weston (Linden Artists) 8–9*b*, 10–11, 26*tl*, 26–27; Encompass Graphics 22–23, 25*tr*, 46*b*

The publisher would also like to thank Ian Harvey for research assistance.

Blackbeard's pirate crew